The Seven Churches of Asia
The Challenge for Faithful Churches
Then and Today

By
Matt Hennecke

ISBN 10: 1-58427-152-3
ISBN 13: 978-1-58427-152-9

Guardian of Truth Foundation
CEI Bookstore
220 S. Marion St., Athens, AL 35611
1-855-49-BOOKS or 1-855-492-6657
www.CEIbooks.com

truth
BOOKS

CONTENTS

Blessed is he who reads and those who hear the words of the prophecy, and heed the things which are written in it...
- Revelation 1:3

The Seven Churches of Asia

Clash of Kingdoms

Lesson 1

The Roman Empire

From its beginnings in the 8th century B.C., Rome grew to dominate the entire Mediterranean region, spreading its language, government, and culture throughout the area.

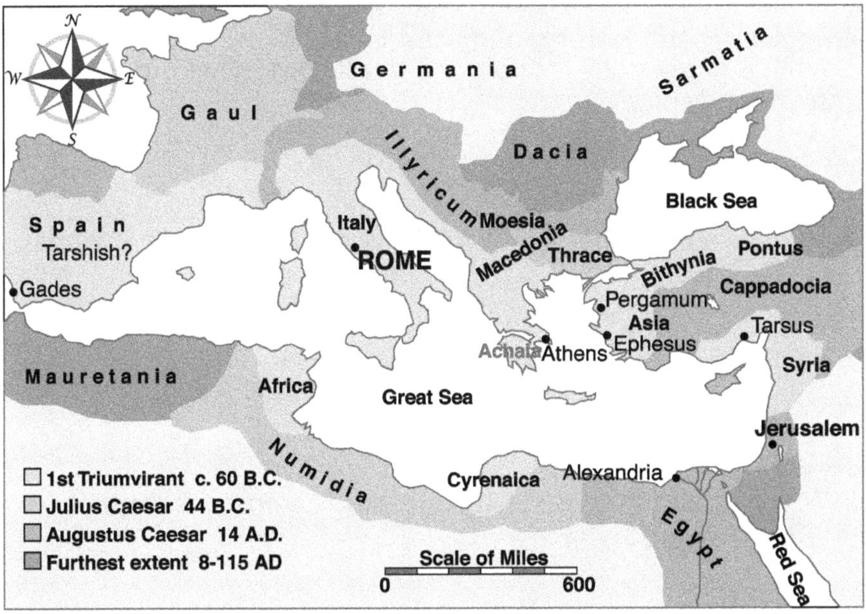

N
W
E
S
Germania
Sarmatia
Gaul
Dacia
Illyricum
Black Sea
Spain
Tarshish?
Gades
Italy
ROME
Moesia
Macedonia
Thrace
Bithynia
Pontus
Cappadocia
Pergamum
Asia
Ephesus
Tarsus
Achaia
Athens
Syria
Mauretania
Africa
Great Sea
Jerusalem
Numidia
Cyrenaica
Alexandria
Egypt
Red Sea
1st Triumvirant c. 60 B.C.
Julius Caesar 44 B.C.
Augustus Caesar 14 A.D.
Furthest extent 8-115 AD
Scale of Miles
0
600

Read Daniel 2:31-49; 7:1-8

1. Nebuchadnezzar had a dream in which he saw a statue, which represented four kingdoms. What is it thought the fourth kingdom represented?

2. What destroyed the statue according to Daniel 2:34? What did that which destroyed the statue become (verse 35)?

3. What is the kingdom that will never be destroyed mentioned in Daniel 2:44-45? (See Luke 1:31-33; Heb.12:28 and Rev. 1:9.)

4. What is it thought the fourth beast of Daniel 7:7-8 represents? What is the *behavior* and *description* of this beast?

Read Revelation 13:1-10

5. What is it generally thought the beast coming up out of the sea represents?

6. What did the people of the earth do according to verses 3-4?

7. What did the beast do to the saints?

8. What, according to verse 10, can stand against the captivity, and the sword?

Ten Great Persecutions

1st Persecution: In approximately A.D. 64 the city of Rome was burned to the ground. Nero was accused of setting the city on fire. He, however, charged the "most despised sect of the Jews" with the crime. Tacitus says, "In order to put down the rumor he set up as objects of accusation and punishment those whom were called Christians." Deaths were numerous. Mockeries were added to their deaths. Some were tied up, wrapped in the skins of wild beasts and torn to pieces by dogs. Still others were crucified while many more were set on fire. It was during this time that the Jews sent Paul for execution.

2nd Persecution: Occurred in the reign of Domitian. Many Christians were condemned for their beliefs—the number put to death is estimated at 40,000.

3rd Persecution: This persecution began in the reign of Trajan about A.D. 100 and lasted for 6 years. Anyone who refused to worship the national gods or indulge in the national vices was put to death.

4th Persecution: Following on the heels of the 3rd persecution, the 4th persecution was perhaps the most cruel lasting for 19 years. Thousands of Christians were separated from their families and tortured and killed.

5th Persecution: This was brought on by Emperor Severus (A.D. 193-211). He issued an edict forbidding anyone to embrace Christianity. During this great persecution a mother and her young daughter were caught and ordered to deny Christ or be boiled alive. Both the mother and daughter remained true to Christ even in their deaths. One of the executioners, so moved by their constancy, became a Christian himself and was later put to death. This persecution lasted 18 years.

6th, 7th, 8th, 9th persecutions over the next several decades. Thousands of Christians died.

10th Persecution: Began in A.D. 302 and lasted for 10 years. Houses where Christians had gathered to worship were sealed and set on fire. On other occasions, many Christians—including their small children—were tied together with ropes, weighted with heavy stones, and thrown into the sea. Seventeen thousand were slain in one month, and the total killed exceeded 140,000.

Read Matt. 4:10, 22:21; Rom. 13:1-7

9. The primary theme of Revelation is the clash between "Caesar" worship and God worship. Who are Christians to worship?

10. What are Christians to render to Caesar and what are they to render to God? What conflict might this cause a Christian?

11. What is a Christian's responsibility to government – even a government that may be corrupt?

Emperor Domitian required all under his reign call him dominus et deus, "lord and god." Failure to do so could result in banishment or death.

Question for Discussion

John's instruction to the seven churches of Asia encouraged them to remain faithful despite persecution. In what ways do you see persecution of Christians in the world today? Be ready to share your thoughts.

The Seven Churches of Asia

John's Vision

Lesson 2

The 7 Churches of Asia

Instructions: Label the location of each of the seven churches of Asia. Label the other churches, according to the Bible, that were in the province of Asia. (Acts 20:6-11; Col. 1:2; 4:13) Circle where John was when he wrote Revelation.

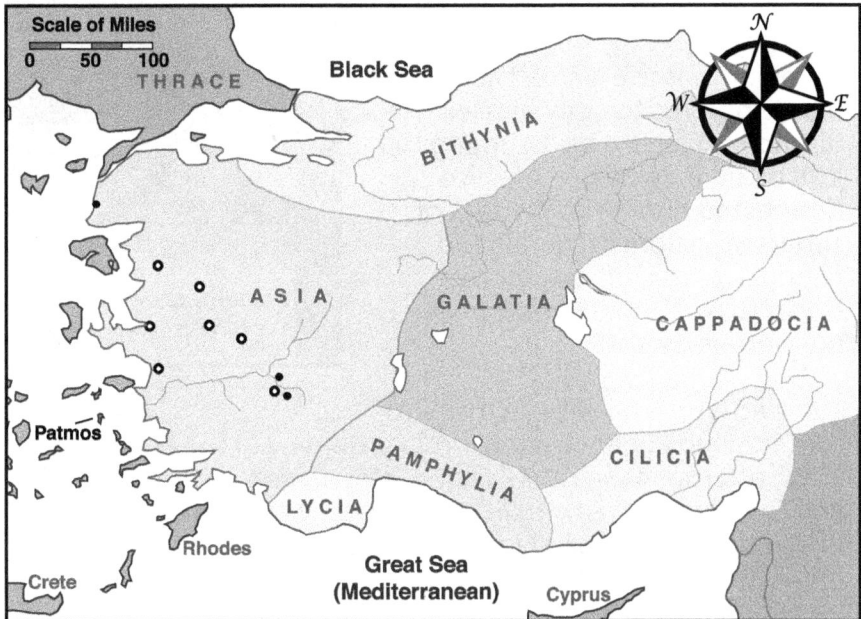

Background

- Established about 130 B.C., the Roman province of Asia should not be confused with the continent of Asia. The province of Asia was the center of emperor worship and it was in the province that the first temples were built to honor the emperors.

- The warnings and instructions to the seven churches of Asia appear in the opening chapters of Revelation, which was written by John. It is generally accepted this "John" was the apostle who also wrote the fourth gospel and the three epistles bearing his name.

- While some debate exists, it is generally believed that Revelation was written about A.D. 95. This date generally coincides with the establishment of Roman law that made it a capital crime to be a Christian.

- It was in the context of growing persecution of the church that John wrote Revelation. With threats from Rome increasing, Christians found themselves having to choose between devotion and obedience to Christ or to the Roman Emperor Domitian (A.D. 81-96).

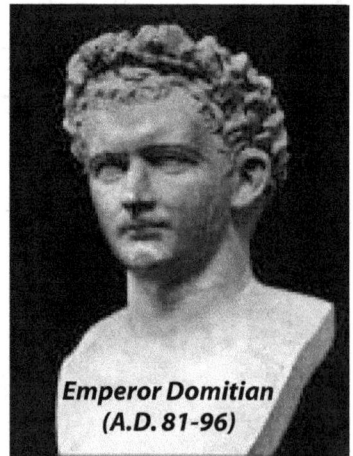

Emperor Domitian (A.D. 81-96)

- Domitian was the first of the Roman emperors to deify himself during his lifetime by assuming the title of "Lord and God." He also nominated himself to the task of supervising Roman morals and conduct, a task difficult for him since his own morals were essentially non-existent.

- Many attempts have been made to turn the book of Revelation into a prophecy of the end of time. Many attempt to see in its pages, references to Napoleon, Hitler, and Saddam Hussein. However, the best way to understand Revelation and the warnings to the seven churches is in the immediate context of the day. It also offers comfort in any age wherein persecution arises against God's people.

📖 Read Revelation 1:1-20

1. Do the opening three verses say anything about the "timing" of the things of which John is writing? What does it say?

2. As priests whom do we serve according to verse 6? Compare to 1 Peter 2:9.

3. List below **all** the things verses 5-7 say about Jesus Christ:

4. In verse 9, what does John say he is a part of that might be viewed as threatening to the Roman Empire?

5. Where was John when he wrote Revelation. Why was he there?

6. List below what John "saw" in his vision (verses 12-16)

7. What do the seven stars represent? What do the seven lampstands represent?

Question for Discussion

What is the significance (if any) of the seven churches being compared to golden lampstands? How might local churches need to be like the lampstands spoken of in Exodus 25:31-40? Be ready to share your thoughts.

Patmos

After being banished to the island of Patmos, the Apostle John was inspired by the Holy Spirit to write Revelation. "I John, who also am your brother, and companion in tribulation, and in the kingdom and patience of Jesus Christ, was in the isle that is called Patmos, for the word of God, and for the testimony of Jesus Christ" (Rev. 1:9). The small, rocky island was used as a place to banish criminals who were forced to work the mines. It is believed that Emperor Domitian banished John to the island about A.D. 95.

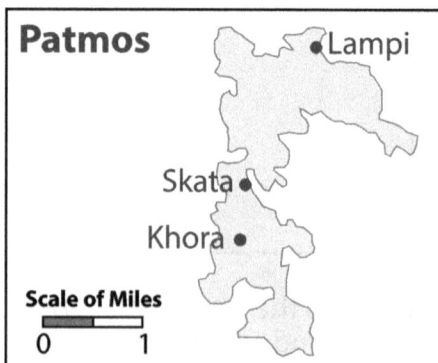

Patmos

Lampi

Skata

Khora

Scale of Miles

0   1

The Seven Churches of Asia

The Living One

Lesson 3

A Modern Parable

The love of your life, the person for whom you have the greatest adoration and affection goes on a journey to a distant land. You lose contact and fear you have lost forever the person for whom you feel you were made and for whom you constantly yearn. As the days turn to weeks, the weeks to months, and the months to years, you fear your love will never return.

At night you are haunted by dread that your love is dead, but on quiet afternoons you are comforted by a journal in which you read about your love and the kindness and generosity which drew you to your love in the first place.

Time marches on, however, and hope begins to fade. Imperceptibly, at first, others begin to vie for your attention. You resist their overtures, but feel yourself drawn to their companionship and love. You want to be true to your love, but you feel the growing ache of loneliness. The memory of your love is growing dim.

Then, one morning a message arrives by a trusted friend. Wonderful news! Your long lost love has been seen! The love of your life is alive, and has sent a message and will be returning!

Instructions: Consider the parable on the previous page as you answer the following questions:

1. How would your disposition and attitude change if you were the recipient of such good news from a trusted messenger?

2. What would you **do** in response to the good news you had received? In other words, how would you *prepare* for the return of your love?

3. How would your ability to handle disappointments, setbacks, and even persecution change as a result of the good news?

Read Revelation 1:4-6, 17-20; 21:2

4. Relate the parable to the words of John about the return of our Lord Jesus. Be prepared to share your observations about the effect John's good news would have on persecuted Christians.

5. What is the relationship of Christ to the church? (See also Matt. 16:15-19; Eph. 1:22-23.)

6. Jesus is described as the "first born of the dead" in verse 5. What does that mean?

7. When Jesus returns, will his return be obscured to most, or will it be evident to all?

8. List below all the verses in chapter one that speak of the *past*, the *present* and the *future*.

9. What does "Alpha and Omega" of verse 8 mean? (See also Isaiah 41:4; 44:6; and 48:12.)

10. What does Christ *have* according to verse 18? What does he accomplish with these? (See v. 5 and 1 Cor. 15:55-58.)

11. What did Jesus say he would *give* to his disciples as recorded in Matthew 16:19? Relate these to Revelation 1:18.

Christic Lives!

The first chapter of Revelation emphasizes the *living* Christ. Jesus is the Son of God who came to the earth, lived a sinless life, and then died for the sins of the world. But, and this is critically important, he was resurrected and **now** lives. Though he died sixty some years *before* John wrote Revelation (A.D. 95-96), he was living when John wrote, and he is living today!

With the looming persecution, John begins by instilling a certain hope to the seven churches because Christ lives.

P.T. Forsyth put it this way: *"We must have the historic Christ and more. We must have the living Christ....He must be our Saviour, in our situation, our needs, loves, shames, sins. He must not only live, but mingle with our lives....We have in Christ...the Reader of our hearts, the Helper of our most private straits, the Inspirer of our most deep and sacred confessions. That is the Christ we need, and, thank God, that is the Christ we have."* (Source: *The Seven Churches of Asia* by James Tolle, page 15.)

Question for Discussion

Revelation is addressed to the seven churches of Asia, but there were more than seven churches in Asia (Troas, Hierapolis, and Colossae and possibly others.) Why was it addressed to these seven and why were the others excluded from this list?

The Seven Churches of Asia

PART 1

Ephesus

Lesson 4

Seven Stars are Seven Angels

In Revelation 1:20 John speaks of "seven stars" which **are** the *angels* of the seven churches. The Greek word for angels is *aggelos* which conveys the idea of "bringing tidings" and literally means "a messenger." Notice that each time John addresses one of the seven churches, he begins with the phrase, *"To the angel of the church...."* Who are these angels? Are they 1) symbolic (if so, what do they symbolize?), 2) spirit beings, or 3) humans?

Symbolic
Some have suggested the term "angel" refers to the ideal, spiritual embodiment of the churches. In other words, churches, while comprised of flesh and blood humans, are primarily spiritual entities and are part of a spiritual kingdom.

Spirit Beings
It has also been argued that the angels are *guardian* spirits. The Bible does seem to suggest guardian angels of nations (Dan. 10:13, 20-21) and even of individuals (Heb. 1:13-14).

Humans
The term angel in the Bible sometimes refers to humans (e.g. "messengers" in Luke 7:24). Could the angels, then, be the spiritual leaders of each of the churches, that is, the elders overseeing each church?

Background

- Ephesus was the capital city of the Roman province of Asia.

- The church at Ephesus was established by Paul on his 2nd missionary journey. Aquila and Priscilla contributed to the growth of the church in Ephesus (Acts 18:18-26).

- Paul returned to Ephesus on his 3rd missionary journey and stayed 2-3 years teaching and performing miracles (Acts 19:8-11; 20:31).

- Ephesus was noted for its worship of the goddess Artemis (Diana). A great temple was built in Ephesus to honor Artemis, which became one of the "Seven Wonders of the Ancient World". Artemis was worshiped mainly as a fertility goddess in Ephesus.

- A great riot occurred in the city of Ephesus caused by Artemis worshippers who clashed with worshippers of Christ (Acts 19:23-41).

Artemis

- Ephesus was a center of emperor worship. Caesar worship was expected of city inhabitants. Failure to comply could result in banishment, property seizure, and/or death.

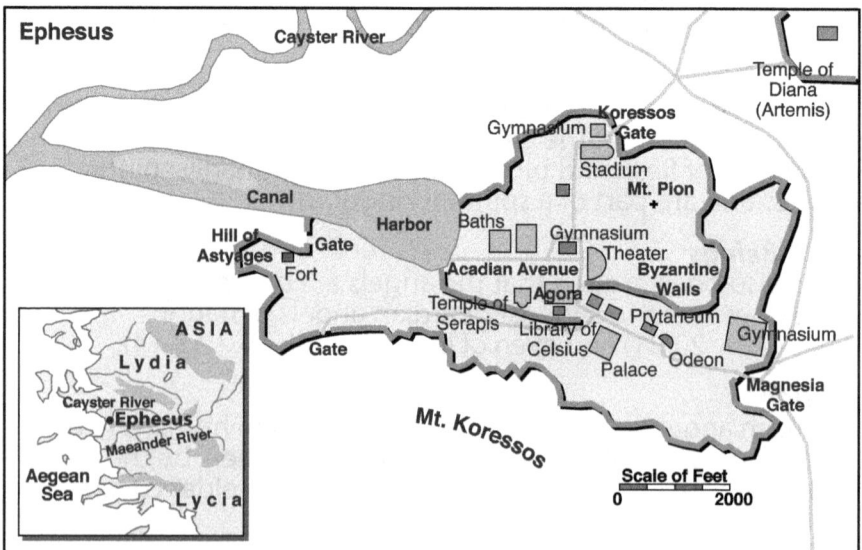

Read Acts 19:8-20, 23-41

1. How far did the teaching of Paul extend? (See Acts 19:10, 26.)

2. What does Acts 19:17, 20 say about the reception of the story of Jesus Christ?

3. What element within the city of Ephesus caused the great riot?

Read Acts 20:17-32

4. What did Paul say was the role of the elders of the church at Ephesus?

5. What warning did Paul give the elders of the church in Ephesus?

Read Ephesians 1:18-23

6. Where is Christ *now*? How does Christ's level of authority compare to that of, say, Rome? Would this assertion cause suspicion on the part of the Roman authorities?

7. Who is the head of the church? What does that mean?

8. Of what are Christians citizens? How might such a concept be viewed by Rome?

9. What statement about God in Ephesians 4:6 might be not play well with the Roman authorities in Ephesus?

10. What is the "evil day" (6:13) which Paul says we must resist by taking up the "full armor of God"?

11. Where was Paul when he wrote Ephesians? (6:20)

Question for Discussion

Which of the three explanations for the "seven angels" (from the front page) do you think is most likely? Do you have a different view of who the angels are? Be ready to share your thinking.

The Seven Churches of Asia

PART 2

Ephesus

Lesson 5

"I KNOW"

Jesus Christ is the the *"One who holds the seven stars in His right hand,"* and is the *"One who walks among the seven golden lampstands"* (Rev. 2:1).

Now consider the first two words of Revelation 2:2: *"I know."* Those two words say much about the deity of our Lord and Savior. As He communicates through John to Ephesus, He reveals He has knowledge not based on rumor, hearsay, or speculation. What He is about to say is <u>fact</u> and there can be no legitimate disagreement from the church in Ephesus.

Read Luke 6:6-10; John 2:23-25

1. Of what was Jesus capable that mere men are not (Luke 6:8)? What do we commonly call this attribute of deity?

2. Summarize what Jesus "knows" about men as revealed in John 2:23-25:

Read Revelation 2:1-7

Praise for the Church

1. List below the *specific* things for which John praises the church in Ephesus:

2. How are churches to "test" whether or not an apostle (i.e. delegate) is telling the truth or not? (See Acts 17:10-11.)

3. What is a local church do if one is found to be false? (See Eph. 5:11; 2 Thess. 3:6, 14)

4. Who were the Nicolaitans?

5. What was the one problem evident in the church at Ephesus?

6. How can a church be praised for 1) perseverance, for 2) dealing with evil men, and for 3) not growing weary, but at the same time be charged with the problem above? Explain.

7. What is the difference between problems of *truth* and problems of the *heart*? Relate your answer to John 4:24. Of which type did the church at Ephesus suffer?

8. Which problem might be more typical of a new convert? Which problem might be more typical of one who has been a Christian for a long time?

9. What instruction does John give the church at Ephesus?

10. From where or what had they fallen? Relate your answer to the marriage relationship imagery in Jeremiah 2:2.

11. What was the church in Ephesus in danger of losing if they failed to repent?

12. How does the local congregation here compare to the church in Ephesus?

Question for Discussion

As he ends his specific advice to the Ephesians, John makes mention of the "tree of life, which is in the Paradise of God" (Rev. 2:7). What tree is this and how do we get access to it?

The Seven Churches of Asia

Smyrna

SMYRNA

Lysimachus, one of Alexander the Great's generals, built Smyrna from the ruins of an earthquake as a Hellenistic city in the 3rd century B.C. The city was later established as a Roman commercial center with a port on the Aegean Sea. The city had a population of 100,000 by the time of the apostles Paul and John.

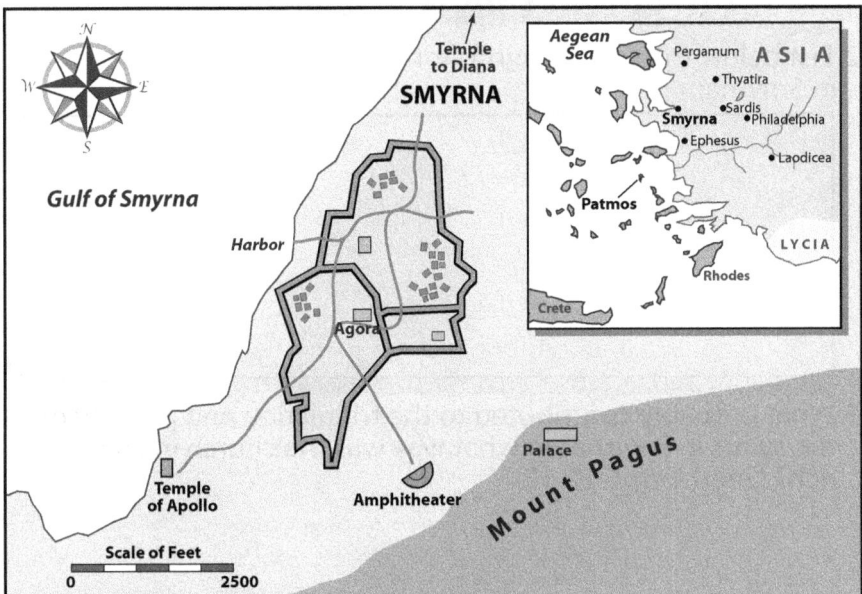

More About Smyrna

• Smyrna was a seaport and commerce center and was widely known for its schools of science and medicine. It was thought to be the most brilliant city in all of Asia, even surpassing Ephesus in splendor.

• The theater in Smyrna was estimated to have seated 20,000 spectators.

• The city had temples devoted to Roman Emperor Tiberias (14-37 A.D.) as well as to the goddess Roma and to the Roman gods Jupiter, Diana, Apollo and others.

• How the church was established is unknown, though it very likely came into being as part of the spread of the gospel from Ephesus. (See Acts 19:10, 26.)

Read Revelation 2:8-11

1. John describes Jesus as the "first and the last, who was dead, and *has come to life*" (2:8). Why might this be encouraging, given John's prophecy for the church in 2:10?

Praise for the Church

2. List below the *specific* things for which John praises the church in Smyrna:

3. What probably contributed to the tribulation and poverty of the saints in Smyrna? In what way was the church in Smyrna rich? (See 1 Tim. 6:17-19)

Problems Confronting the Church

4. The church in Smyrna received praise from John without a single word of censure. Nevertheless, there was a big problem about to confront them. What was that big problem?

Read 2 Corinthians 4:8-10, 16-18

5. Based on verses 8-9, complete the following chart:

	but not	
	but not	
	but not	
	but not	

6. Now consider Paul's words of comfort for the persecuted as you complete the following chart based on verses 16-18:

	Duration	Intensity
Earthly affliction		
Heavenly bliss		

7. Have you ever suffered persecution for Christ? If so, how were you persecuted? Is persecution inevitable for Christians? (See John 15:20.)

8. What does John encourage the church in Smyrna to do in the face of looming persecution? What will they receive for their fidelity?

9. What does Romans 8:35-39 say about persecution and the love of the Lord?

10. What is the "second death" mentioned in Rev. 2:11? (See Rev. 21:8.)

Question for Discussion

John uses harsh language to describe blasphemous Jews. He says they are a "synagogue of Satan" (Rev. 2:9). What does that mean?

The Seven Churches of Asia

Pergamum

7 Lesson

PERGAMUM

Pergamum: (Pergamos) Hellenistic Pergamum is considered the most important city of ancient Mysia. It is located about 3 miles north of the Caicus River and sat at an elevation of about 1,300 feet, the city itself having been built on a series of terraces.

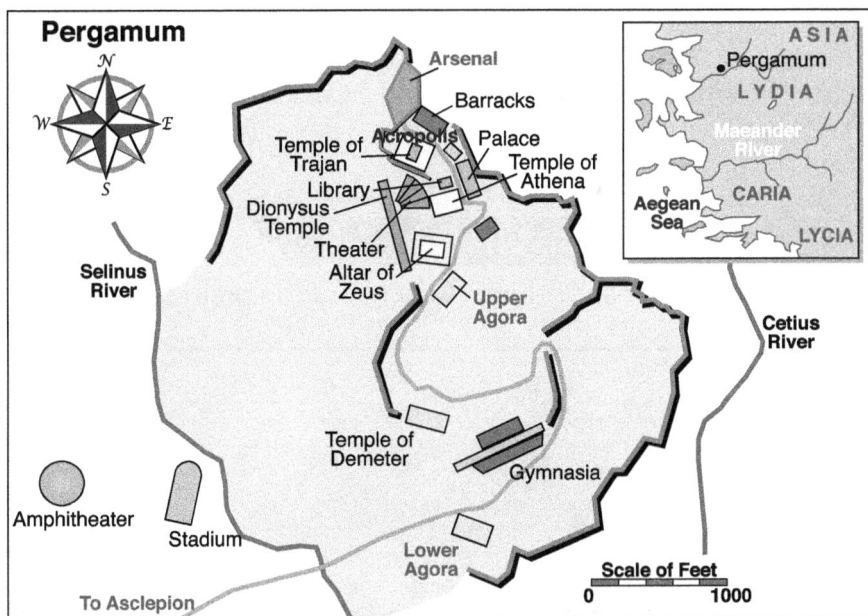

Pergamum

Arsenal
Barracks
Palace
Temple of Trajan
Temple of Athena
Acropolis
Library
Dionysus Temple
Theater
Altar of Zeus
Upper Agora
Selinus River
Temple of Demeter
Gymnasia
Cetius River
Amphitheater
Stadium
Lower Agora
To Asclepion

ASIA
Pergamum
LYDIA
Maeander River
Aegean Sea
CARIA
LYCIA

Scale of Feet
0   1000

More About Pergamum

• The city was known for its wealth and devotion to fashion.

• Pergamum is credited with first making parchment (Latin: *pergamena*) and was known as an educational and cultural center in the Roman province of Asia.

• The city library at one time held over 200,000 volumes, but most of the works were given by Mark Antony to Cleopatra for the library in Alexandria, Egypt.

• The city and its inhabitants were idolatrous with statues to many gods including an impressive altar devoted to Zeus. Other temples were erected to Athena and Dionysus, the god of wine. Emperor worship began in Pergamum.

• The church in Pergamum very likely came into existence as a result of Paul's work in Ephesus (Acts 19:10, 26).

Read Revelation 2:12-17

1. What is Jesus described as having as John begins his address to the church in Pergamum? What is the significance of this? (See Rev. 1:16; Heb. 4:12.)

2. Where, according to John, does the church in Pergamum dwell (2:13)? What does this mean? (See 2 Cor. 6:14-18.)

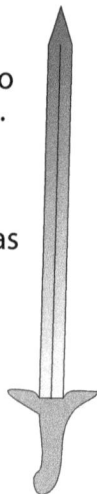

Praise for the Church

3. List below the *specific* things for which John praises the church in Pergamum:

4. Who was a member of the Lord's church in Pergamum at one time and was killed for his faithfulness?

Secular history suggests a certificate may have been issued as proof of emperor allegiance.

〈ᕮRTIFI〈ATᕮ

Problems in the Church

5. What specific problems does John say existed in the church at Pergamum? List them below:

Read Numbers 22:5-6; 25:1-3; 2 Peter 2:15-16

6. Through his counsel to Balak, Balaam was responsible for the "stumbling block" which led to Israel's sin. What specific sins did Israel commit? (See Num. 25:1-3.)

7. What is idolatry, and can idolatry be present in the Lord's church today? Explain.

8. What happens to a local church if false teaching is allowed? (See 1 Cor. 5:6-7.) According to Romans 16:17-18 what should be done about false teachers?

Prescription for the Church

9. What is John's prescription for the evil influences that have infiltrated the church in Pergamum?

What warning is given should they fail to repent?

10. What are the specific promises to those of Pergamum who overcome?

Question for Discussion

What is meant by the three things promised to those who overcome? Consider John 6:31-35, the symbolism of "white," and Isaiah 62:2.

The Seven Churches of Asia

Thyatira

Lesson 8

Thyatira

Thyatira was a wealthy city that sat on the River Lycus and served as an important commercial route between Pergamum to the northwest and Sardis to the south. More trade guilds were known to exist in Thyatira than in any other Asian city. Trades included wool and linen workers, makers of garments, dyers, leather workers, tanners, potters, bakers, slave traders and bronze smiths. Lydia, the seller of purple taught by Paul in Philippi, was from Thyatira (Acts 16:14). According to James Tolle, every tradesman was part of a guild and the guilds were closely tied to idol worship.

The church in Thyatira likely came into existence as a result of Paul's efforts in Ephesus (See Acts 19:10, 26.)

More About Thyatira

- The heathen guardian of the city was the god, Tyrimnos, who has been identified with the Greek sun god Apollo. Tyrimnos was connected with the guilds. If you were a craftsmen, you were expected to join a guild and to honor Tyrimnos as well as the other pagan gods.

Apollo, the sun god

- The dilemma facing craftsmen who converted to Christianity was that obedience to Christ very likely meant the loss of their livelihood and financial resources.

- There is debate about the meaning of the city name. Some suggest the name comes from the Greek *thauteria* meaning "castle of Thya." Other's believe the name of the city is associated with Jezebel and originates from the Greek *thea,* "a female deity, goddess," and *tyrannos,*" a tyrant or ruler." Others believe Thyatira is a variation on the name of the city of Tyre. Both cities worshipped the sun god and were known for their purple dyes and guilds.

Read Revelation 2:18-29

1. Who does John say is communicating these words to the church in Thyatira (vs. 18)?

Praise for the Church

2. List below the *specific* things for which John praises the church in Thyatira:

3. What admirable trait evident in Thyatira was missing in the church in Ephesus?

4. How did the works (deeds) of the church in Thyatira change over time? Relate your answer to the need for growth as indicated by Paul in Ephesians 4:14-16.

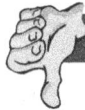

Problems in the Church

5. What specific problems does John say existed in the church at Thyatira? List them below:

Read 1 Kings 16:31-33; 18:13, 19; 21:25-26; 2 Kings 9:30-37

6. Based on the verses above, describe Jezebel's a) character, b) influence, and c) her demise.

a) Her Character:

b) Her Influence over King Ahab:

c) Her Demise:

7. How is the Lord's patience demonstrated even in the case of one as bad as this Jezebel of Thyatira?

8. What is Lord's prescription for the evil influences of Jezebel which have infiltrated the church in Thyatira?

What warning is given to those who fail to repent?

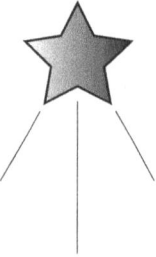

9. What is the "morning star" promised to the faithful (Rev. 22:16)?

Question for Discussion

Is the Jezebel mentioned and described an actual woman or a characterization of a faction that encouraged immorality in Thyatira?

The Seven Churches of Asia

Sardis

Lesson 9

Sardis

The ancient city of Sardis lies in the Hermus valley at an altitude of about 310 feet above sea level. The acropolis to the south, in the Tmolus range, was another thousand feet higher, at an altitude of about 1,340 feet above sea level.

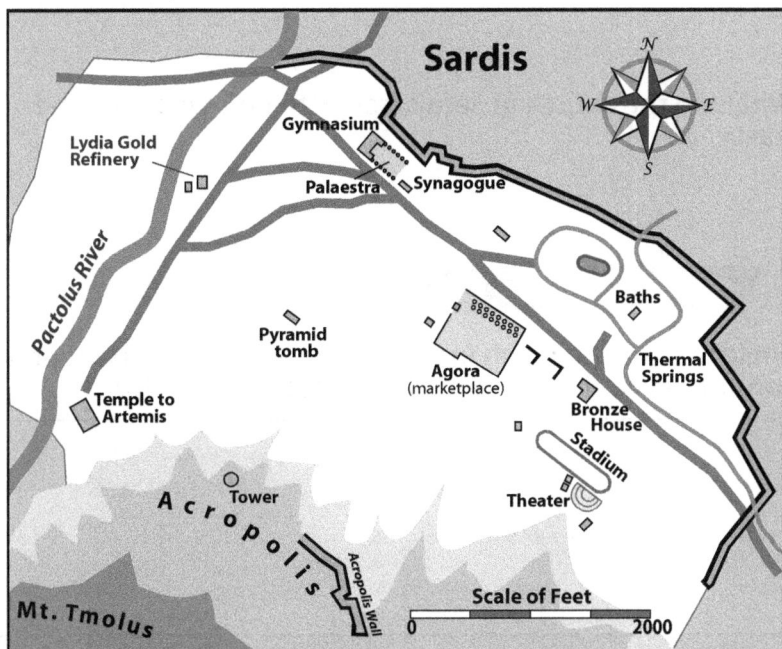

Sardis

Lydia Gold Refinery
Gymnasium
Palaestra
Synagogue
Pactolus River
Pyramid tomb
Agora (marketplace)
Baths
Temple to Artemis
Bronze House
Thermal Springs
Stadium
Tower
Theater
Acropolis
Acropolis Wall
Mt. Tmolus
Scale of Feet
0   2000

More About Sardis

• The ancient city of Sardis had sheer walls on three sides which made the city virtually impregnable to attack. However, the area is prone to earthquakes and in A.D. 17 the city was destroyed by earthquake and rebuilt.

• Sardis was known for its wealth and was a trade center when it was the capital of the Kingdom of Lydia. Gold mines nearby increased the wealth of the city. Sardis is credited with minting the first coins in history in the 7th century B.C.

• Sardis was the last stop on the famous Royal Road which started in Susa, over 1,600 miles to the southeast.

• The Artemis temple area is 160 by 200 feet in size, making it one of the largest temples in the Greek world.

• The church was likely established when the gospel spread from the efforts of the apostle Paul while in Ephesus (Acts 19:10, 26.)

Read Revelation 3:1-6

1. What is the Lord described as *having* in verse 1? (See Rev. 1:4, 16.)

2. What did the church in Sardis "seem" to be? What was the reality? (vs. 1)

Praise for the Church

3. While there is not much in the church worthy of commendation, list below the few positive attributes of the church:

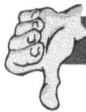

4. What is the Lord's assessment of the spiritual "alertness" of the church in Sardis? Relate their condition to Paul's warning in 1 Thessalonians 5:1-11.

5. What might be the telltale signs of "spiritual stupor" in the Lord's church today? Make a list of possible symptoms:

6. In addition to their problem above, what other problems existed in the church at Sardis? List them below:

7. What was the indicator that some in Sardis were still in good standing with the Lord (v. 4)?

8. Read Isaiah 1:16-20 and relate its message to the condition of most of the Christians in Sardis.

Prescription for the Church

9. What is the Lord's prescription for what ails most of the saints in Sardis?

10. What is the threefold promise given to those who repent and remain faithful to the Lord?

Question for Discussion

What exactly is the "book of life" mentioned in Revelation 3:5? Can we infer our name is listed in it until such time as we sin? What do Philippians 4:3 and Revelation 20:15 say about this "book"?

The Seven Churches of Asia

Philadelphia

Philadelphia

King Attalus Philadelphus II of Pergamum built the city out of affection for his brother Ecumenes II – hence the name "Philadelphia" which literally means "city of brotherly love."

More About Philadelphia

• Located on the main route between east and west, Philadelphia was a wealthy trade city known for its vineyards and farming. Not surprisingly, the city had many festivals dedicated to the god Dionysus (Bacchus), the Greek god of wine and intoxication.

• In A.D. 17 an earthquake destroyed Philadelphia. Sardis, to the northwest, suffered worse damage from the initial quake, but Philadelphia suffered through several, severe aftershocks, which terrified the population. Because of the earthquake threat, many of the inhabitants refused to live in the city but instead lived in small farm houses outside the city. Emperor Tiberius assisted in reconstruction of the city and for a time the city was called "Neocaesarea" (new Caesar) as a tribute to the assistance from Rome.

• Such was the devotion to idol worship that by the 3rd century the city came to be known as "little Athens."

• As with most of the seven churches, the Philadelphia church was likely established when the gospel spread from the efforts of the apostle Paul while in Ephesus (Acts 19:10, 26.)

Read Revelation 3:7-13

1. What specific description is given of the One addressing the church in Philadelphia in verse 7?

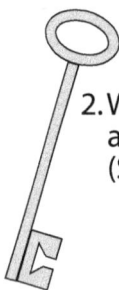

2. What idea is conveyed by reference to the "key of David" and what does the Lord open and shut using the key? (See Matt. 16:18-19.)

3. What has the Lord put before the church that no one can shut? What does this mean? (See Acts 14:27, 1 Cor. 16:8-9, Col. 4:2-4.)

What doors of opportunity exist for the church here? Think about it.

Praise for the Church

4. List below the specific praise the Lord has for the church in Philadelphia:

5. Because the church kept the word, what does the Lord say he will keep from them?

Problems in the Church

6. Do any problems exist *inside* the church in Philadelphia? Are there challenges facing the church from *outside*?

7. What is the "synagogue of Satan" (v. 9)? What will hypocritical Jews ultimately *do* and ultimately *know*? (See Isaiah 60:14.)

Prescription for the Church

8. The church in Philadelphia is doing well, however the Lord still provides what prescription to them?

9. What specific promises does the Lord make to those who continue stedfast in the faith?

Question for Discussion

The Lord says to those who remain faithful that he will "make him a pillar in the temple of God." What does the image of a "pillar" signify?

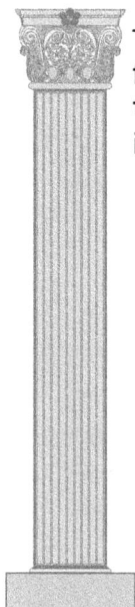

The Seven Churches of Asia

Laodicea

Lesson 11

Laodicea

Laodicea was founded about 250 B.C. by Antiochus II of Syria, and was named after his wife Laodice who according to history later poisoned him. The city sat on the main road between Ephesus to the west and Syria to the east. It was known as a great financial and manufacturing center.

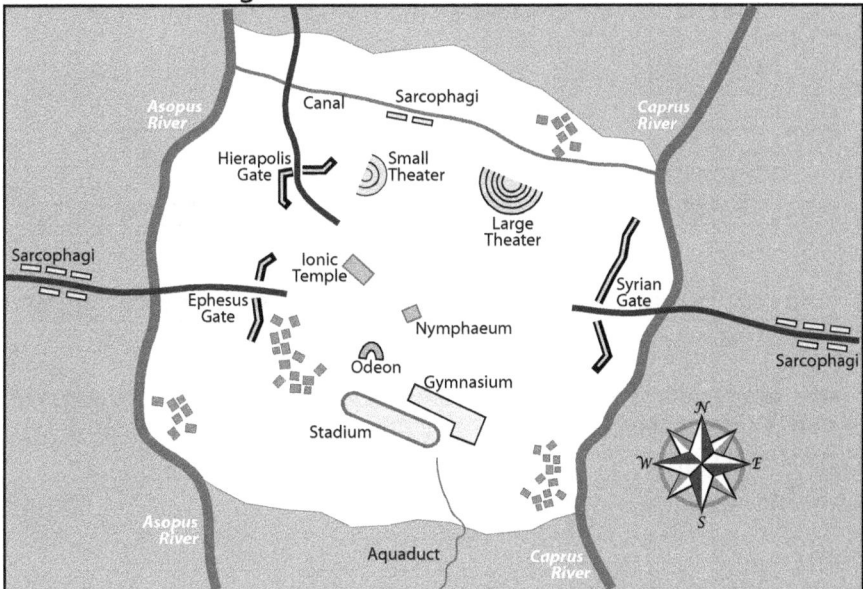

More About Laodicea

• The city of Laodicea was notable for its interest in medicine and in particular for its use of *collyrium*, an ointment used in the treatment of eye diseases.

• The city was also known for the high quality black wool it produced and sold throughout Asia and beyond.

• The city was a wealthy banking and financial center. Such was the great wealth of the city, that when it was destroyed by earthquake in A.D. 61. it declined help from Rome in reconstruction.

• Hot springs in the city of Hierapolis to the north flowed southward but were luke warm by the time they reached the city of Laodicea.

• While the church may have been established by the spread of the gospel from Ephesus (Acts 19:10, 26), it has been suggested that Epaphras—a member of the church in Colossae—may have had a part in its establishment. The churches in Laodicea, Colossae and Hierapolis apparently enjoyed a warm relationship (Col. 4:12-15).

• A letter written by Paul to the church in Laodicea has been lost in antiquity (Col. 4:16).

Read Revelation 3:14-22

1. As John begins writing to the church in Laodicea, what three phrases are used to describe Christ?

2. What does the word "amen" mean? How does its meaning relate to Christ?

3. What is meant by Jesus being the "Beginning of the creation"? Is this a reference to the *physical* creation or to the church–a *spiritual* creation? (See Col 1:16-17,18-23.)

spiritual creation

physical creation

Praise for the Church

4. Does the Lord have any praise at all for the church in Laodicea? If so, what is praiseworthy?

Problems in the Church

5. What is the spiritual condition of the church in Laodicea?

6. What two spiritual conditions does the Lord indicate would be preferable?

7. In what ways would being *cold* be preferable to being luke-warm? List some ways below:

8. In what way did the Laodiceans feel themselves to be rich (v. 17)? What clue does Mark 4:18-19 give to the likely cause of their spiritual condition?

9. What five terms are used to describe the *reality* of their situation (vs. 17)?

They were _____

They were _____

They were _____

They were _____

They were _____

Prescription for the Church

10. What three things does the Lord advise they "buy" from Him and for what purpose?

11. What two promises are made to the Laodiceans if they will repent, "open the door" to Him, and overcome?

Question for Discussion

The Lord prefers true believers who are "hot." The Greek word for "hot" is *zestos* and in context means "fervent" or "zealous." List below what you believe to be three indicators of "hot" Christians:

1. _____

_____

2. _____

_____

3. _____

_____

The Seven Churches of Asia

The Holy City

Lesson 12

An Eternal and Glorious City for the Faithful

Our study of the seven churches of Asia has focused on the first three chapters; however, we must not overlook the rest of John's prophecy. The first three chapters *specifically* address the issues of the seven churches, but the remaining chapters were directed to and read by those same churches. The rest of the Revelation continues the warnings of persecution, but also conveys a glorious message of hope for those faithful to Christ Jesus.

The seven churches of our study existed in seven cities of Asia: Ephesus, Smyrna, Pergamum, Thyatira, Sardis, Philadelphia, and Laodicea. Another city–a more glorious and eternal city–is also described in the book of Revelation. That city is a holy city–whose builder and maker is God.

For the early Christians of Asia who lived in the midst of rampant evil, the promise of a holy city, a heavenly home must have provided great solace and encouragement. We should be encouraged as well, for we too live in a corrupt and evil world. Like the saints in Asia we must remain faithful to our Lord and Savior.

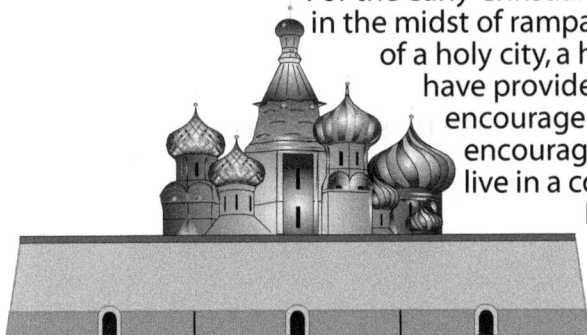

More About the Holy City

• The holy city is the same city Abraham was seeking. It is a city whose architect and builder is God (Heb. 11:8-10).

• While Abraham and other faithful men and women of the Old Testament died without receiving the promises – though they could see them from a distance – God prepared a city for them as well as all who are faitful (Heb. 11:13-16).

• The holy city, the new Jerusalem, is promised by the Lord to those who persevere during times of trial and who overcome (Rev. 3:12; 22:14).

• The city prepared for us is eternal. It will not suffer destruction as did many of the cities of Asia. The Bible refers to it as a "lasting city" (Heb. 13:14).

Read Revelation 21:1-8

1. To what does John compare the holy city in Revelation 21:2?

2. Who will dwell *amongst* the saints when the holy city comes from heaven? How is the holy city described in verse 3?

3. List below all that will cease when the holy city comes (v. 4):

4. What is promised in verse 6 to those who thirst? Relate this promise to Jesus' statements to the Samaritan woman revealed in John 4:7-14.

5. Who will **not** be part of the holy city or drink the water of life?

Read Revelation 21:9-21

6. How many gates are in the wall of the holy city, and what is written on the gates? What do the gates and the names on the gates seem to suggest?

7. How many foundation stones are in the wall of the holy city and what is written on them? How do you interpret this imagery?

8. What is *most* impressive to you about the description of the holy city? Be ready to share your thoughts.

Read Revelation 21:22-27

9. Is there a temple in the holy city? Why or why not?

10. Who will be the light source in the heavenly city?

Read Revelation 22:1-15

11. What flows through the holy city and what is on either side?

12. How will the Lord "mark" those who are His (v. 4)?

13. What condition is placed on those who desire to enter the holy city (v. 14)?

Question for Discussion

Is the holy city described "as a bride adorned for her husband" (Rev. 21:2) the church? If so, why does it seem to appear at the end of time? Wasn't the church established on the day of Pentecost (Acts 2)? Explain.

The Seven Churches of Asia

Lessons for Us

Lesson 13

All scripture is given by inspiration of God, and is profitable for doctrine, for reproof, for correction, for instruction in righteousness: that the man of God may be perfect, thoroughly furnished unto all good works.
- 2 Timothy 3:16 -17

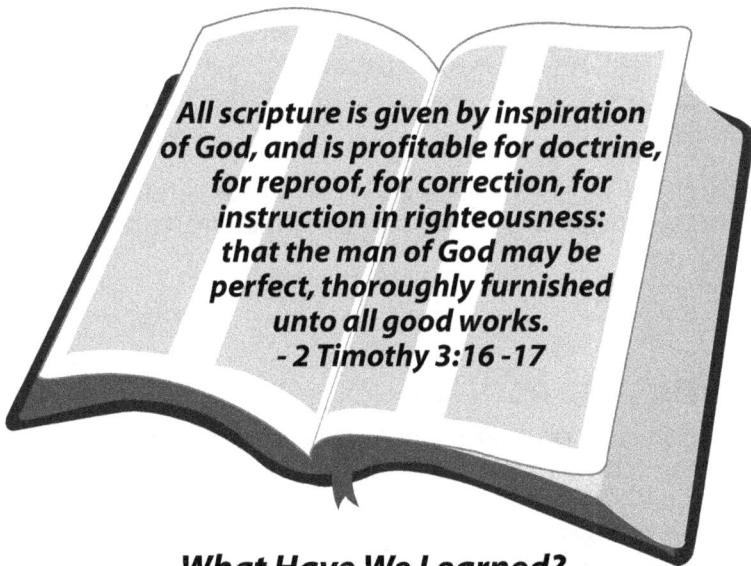

What Have We Learned?

As our study comes to a conclusion, it is a good idea to summarize what we have learned about the seven churches of Asia and to consider the local church of which we are a part. As we learned in our study of the churches of Asia threats can arise from *within* and *outside* a local church. We must be ever watchful for such threats and careful to ensure the church of which we are a part remains unspotted by the world (James 1:27).

Review Revelation Chapters 2 - 3

Review chapters two and three of Revelation and then complete the chart on the next page. A single word or phrase should be sufficient for each box. When you have completed the chart, answer the questions below:

1. Which church seems to have received the *most* praise?

2. Which churches had problems arising from *within* and which churches were confronting problems originating *outside* the congregation?

3. What is the *repeated* prescription for all the churches which were having problems?

4. According to 2 Corinthians 7:9-11 what leads to repentance? List below the *specific* fruits of repentance described in verse 11.

Making Application

5. What potential problems might threaten the local congregation of which you are a part? Are the potential threats internal or external? Be ready to share your thoughts.

Internal Threats	External Threats

7 Churches of Asia - Summary Chart

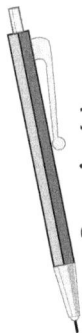

	Praise	Problem(s)	Prescription	Promise(s)
EPHESUS				
SMYRNA				
PERGAMUM				
THYATIRA				
SARDIS				
PHILADELPHIA				
LAODICEA				

6. What specific actions can a Christian take to help a local church remain faithful to the Lord? Suggest at least three ideas and be ready to share them:

> [ ]

> [ ]

> [ ]

Read Revelation 22:16-21

7. How does Jesus describe Himself in verse 16?

8. To whom is the "water of life" offered?

Question for Discussion

Was the message to the churches of Asia speaking of events that took place in the days of his original readers (preterist view), or is the prophecy regarding the end of time yet to come (futurist view)? See Rev. 22:10,20 and Daniel 8:26.